JOHN DENVER

Seasons of the Heart

Associate Music Editor — Dan Fox

Art Direction — Randi Glauberman

ISBN 0-89524-159-5

Edited by Milton Okun

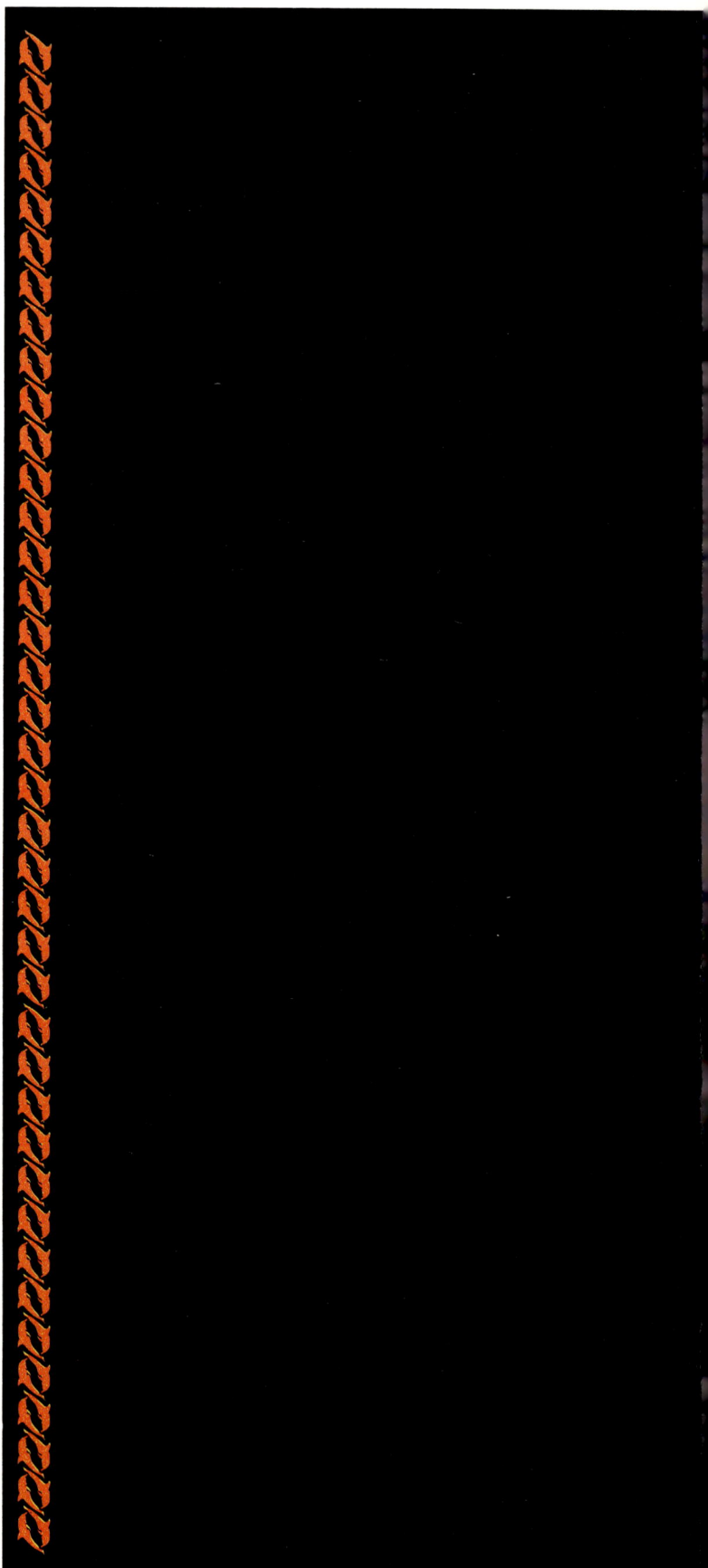

Contents

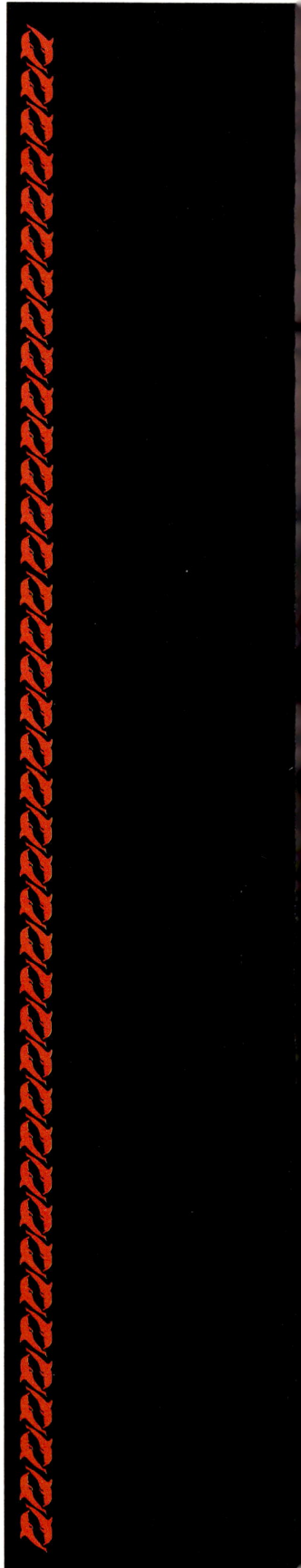

Performance Notes

It's always good news for lovers of good, melodic songs in general and Denver fans in particular when John comes out with a new album. This music book, based on his latest release **SEASONS OF THE HEART** is no exception. The eleven songs in it are fine examples of pop music at its best, and you don't need an elaborate studio production or a 50 piece orchestra to sound good with these songs! Just a piano or guitar accompaniment is enough for a professional sounding performance.

The arrangements are all faithfully transcribed as to key and routine and can be played along with the recorded versions of the songs. Vocalists can easily find the melody in these two-staff arrangements as it is always the top line in the right hand of the piano part unless otherwise marked. They will be pleased to note that all the nuances of John's singing style are accurately reproduced including the slurs and grace notes so often used by country-oriented singers. Pianists and other keyboard players will find that, although the arrangements sound professional and are easy to play as written, enough information is contained in them to give more ambitious players the option of constructing far more elaborate versions if desired. Guitarists, too, will be pleased with the care taken in printing the chord diagrams. Songs like *Seasons Of The Heart*, *Relatively Speaking* and others are in good keys for guitar, and the diagrams give appropriate chord fingerings. On the other hand, *Shanghai Breezes*, *Islands*, *Heart To Heart*, and *Opposite Tables* lie better if the guitar chords are played a whole step lower than the piano chords. To this end, we include directions for placing a capo across the 2nd fret and playing from the upper set of chord symbols in italic type. This allows the guitarist to play in his best sounding key while still being able to play along with the record and the printed piano part. Also, please note that each chord diagram is individually engraved so that the progressions flow logically and smoothly, and are full sounding and easy to play.

Because of the songs, we know this folio will appeal to John Denver's thousands of fans. Because of the quality, it will appeal to contemporary singers, pianists, and guitarists at all levels of musical attainment.

Seasons Of The Heart

Slowly

Words and Music by
John Denver

Of

course, we have our dif-f'renc-es, you should-n't be sur-prised;_ It's as
don't know how to tell_ you, it's dif-fi-cult_ to say,_ I

nat-u-ral_ as chang-es in the sea-sons and the skies.__ Some-
nev-er in_ my wild-est dreams im-ag-ined it this way. Some-

times we grow to-geth-er, some-times we drift a-part;_ A
times I just don't know you, there's a stran-ger in our home;_ When I'm

(2nd time)

wis - er man_ than I _ might know the | sea - sons of the heart._ | And I'm
ly - ing right_ be - side_ you ___ is | when I'm most a - lone._ | And I

walk - ing __ here be - side you _ in the | ear - ly eve - ning chill, | A
think my_ heart is brok - en,_ there's an | emp - ti - ness in - side, | So

thing we've al - ways loved_ to do, I __ | know we al - ways will._ | We
man - y things_ I've longed_ for have so | of - ten been de - nied._ Still I, | I

have so much in com - mon, so | man - y things_ we share, | That I
would - n't try to change you, there's | no one that's_ to blame, | It's

(2nd time)

7

can't be - lieve__ my heart__ when it im - plies that you're not there.__
just some - things__ that mean__ so much, we just don't feel the same.__

Love is why__ I came here__ in the first place,

Love is now__ the rea - son I __ must go,

Love is all__ I ev - er hoped__ to find here,__

Love is still the on-ly dream — I know. _____

F   G   1. C

F   C   G7

— (Spoken) And so I

2. C   F   G

know. _____ True love is still the on-ly dream — I

slower

C   F   C

know. _____

in tempo

Opposite Tables

Words and Music by
John Denver

Moderately

Guitar → A
(Capo up 2 frets)
Piano → B

tuned drum - continue this pattern throughout song

mf

D
E

A
B

A
B

1. Fa - ther, oh Fa - ther, please hear___ me,___ My

song is a cry___ of des - per - a - tion;

All of the words— I hear— have lost— their— mean-

ing. _____ My life is a well— of con-fu-

sion— drowned out by the sound— of the lost—

—and lone - ly; On - ly the voice— in - side—

speaks your name to me.

Chorus

If they only knew the things that I know,

If they only could see the things that I

see.

If they only knew

the things___ that I ___ know,___

E7

F#7

If they on - ly could see the things.that I see.___

A

1.(Hum)___
2. Broth - ers at op - po - site ta - bles,___ Like

fire___ and wa - ter a - gainst___ each oth - er.

Only a fool ___ can't see ___ the ob - vi - ous end-
ing. _____ Are we as ash - es to wild-
wood? ___ Is life just a fire ___ that can on -
ly con - sume ___ us? Is there no vis - ion of love ___

14

to bind us — to-geth - er?

Chorus

If they on - ly knew — the things — that I — know, —

You are on - ly ev-

'ry - thing that I know — If they on - ly could see the things that I

see. —

My

D.S. al Coda

If they on - ly knew___ the things___ that I___

You are on - ly ev - 'ry - thing that I know.__
know,___

If they on - ly could see the things___ that I

Repeat and fade

Ooh___

see.

16

Relatively Speaking

Words by
Arthur Hancock
Music by
John Denver

Moderately

mf

smoothly

C

Rel - a - tive - ly speak - ing, you make me who I am.
Rel - a - tive - ly speak - ing, the con - trast makes it go.

sim.

I need you ex - act - ly like the o -
Ev - 'ry ac - tion tak - en is re - lat -

F

cean needs the land.
ed in the flow.

Am

I need you like sun -
Stars and los - ers, kings

shine   needs   the shad   - ows   and __ the   night. __
__ and   fools   go   danc   - ing   hand __ in   hand, __

I   need   you __   the way __   love   needs   the   sav   - age   hurt - ful
Rel - a - tive - ly   speak - ing,   you make __   me   who   I

fight.
am.

Rel - a - tive - ly   speak-
(Instrumental) __

ing,   I'm   noth - ing   with - out   you. __

You are where I've been be - fore, you are where I'm go - ing to.

You are liv - ing out my dreams and

you are all my fears. You e - voke my laugh-

ter, you un - leash ev - 'ry tear. The
The

Am

rich ones need the poor ones;
sick ones need the well ones;
The

Em

F **G7** **C**

blind need those with sight,
liv - ing need those with the dead.

Am **F**

Sin - ners need the pure of heart;
Heav - en needs its pure hell you know,
The
And

D7 **G** **G7**

black ones need the white.
love needs lone - ly beds.

Rel - a - tive - ly speak - ing, the con - trast makes it go. ___

___ Ev -'ry ac - tion tak - en is re - lat -

ed in ___ the flow. ___ Stars and los - ers, kings ___

___ and fools ___ go danc - ing hand in hand. ___

Rel - a - tive - ly speak - ing, you make me who I am,

who I am.

Du du du du etc.

Repeat and fade

23

Dreams

Words and Music by
Stephen Geyer

Moderately slow

1. There are dreams that sail away to sea,
cor - ner bar the lo - cal star des-

dreams that stay at home;
troys a pass - ing chord;
There are dreams in need of com-
He sits be - hind a ma-

pa - ny, some that stand a - lone. There are
son - jar and dreams of his re - ward. Then he

dreams that stay _____ in - side _____ all _____ day _____ and a
takes his break, _____ he counts _____ his _____ take; a

nev - er see _____ the light, _____ Then if dreams _____ come true _____ I swear. _____
dol - lar buys _____ a beer. _____ A quar - ter of _____ his life _____

_____ to you, _____ I'll dream of you _____ to - night. *(smoothly)*
_____ is gone; _____ What's he do - in'

1.

2.

In the here? Now

times are hard,__ the old back - yard__ is bur - ied in __ ce - ment.__

The peo - ple seem__ a - fraid__ to dream,__ and

dreams don't cost__ a cent.

slower

(solo)

in tempo

N.C.

There are
dreams that stay___ in - side___ all___ day, and
nev - er see___ the light.___ And if dreams___ come true___ I swear___
___ to you___ I'll dream of you___ to -

night.   And if dreams___ come true___ I

swear   to   you   I'll   dream   of   you___   to - night.___

slowing

freely

(solo)
in tempo

N.C.

Nothing But A Breeze

Words and Music by
Jesse Winchester

Moderately

1.3. Life is just too short for some folks; for oth-er folks it just drags
2. Some-day I'll be your great- grand-pa; all the pret-ty girls'll call me

on. Some folks like the taste of smok - ey whis-key;
"sir." Now when they're ask - in' me how things are;

oth-ers fig-ure tea's too strong. I'm the kind-a guy who likes to
soon they'll ask me how things were. I don't mind be - in' an

stand___ in the mid - dle;___ I don't like all this bounc-in' back and
old___ great - grand-pa___ as long as you'll be my great - grand-

forth.
ma. And I think we should move with our___ tea and cook-ies to the

Me, I want to live with my___ feet in Dix - ie and my

head in the cool blue north.___
shade of the old blue pau pau.___ *(last time) I said,*

In a small sub - ur - ban gar - den not a sin - gle neigh-bor knows our
*(Instrumental)*___

name; I know that the wom-an wish-es we could move where the

hous-es are-n't all the same.___ "Say, John-ny, I would like to go to where the

grass is green-er; I could-n't real-ly say___ where it might___ be, But

some-place high___ on a ___ moun-tain top ___ down by the deep blue sea." There we'll do just as we please, ('cause) it ain't noth-in' but a breeze. cool breeze. Me, I want to live with my feet in Dix-ie and my head in the cool blue north.

* Final instrumental fade omitted

33

What One Man Can Do

Words and Music by
John Denver

Slowly

1. I sup - pose____ that there are those____ who'll say he had it eas - y, ____ had it made in fact be - fore he'd e - ven be - gun. But they don't know____ the things I know, I was al - ways with him; It

sim.

* Guitarists:
Play chords fingerstyle

34

may sound strange,— we were more than friends.— 2. It's

hard to tell the truth when no one wants— to lis - ten, When

no one real - ly cares_what's go - in' on. ___ And it's hard to stand a - lone_ when you

need some - one be - side_ you; Your spir - it and your faith must be strong. What one man can do is dream. What one man can do is

more rhythmically

mf

love.___ What one man can do is change the world and make it young a-gain.___
What one man can do is change the world and make it new a-gain.___

To Coda

Here you see___ what one man can do.

3. As

shad - ed as___ his eyes__ might be,   that's how bright_ his mind_ is,

That's how strong his love__ for you and   me.

A

friend to all the u - ni - verse,__ grand-   fa - ther of the fu - ture

D.S. al Coda

ev - 'ry - thing__ that I__ would like to be.__   What

do. What one man can do is dream, What

one man can do is love.____ What one man can do is change the

world and make it work a - gain;___ Here you see___ what one man can

do.

slower

Shanghai Breezes

Slowly

Words and Music by
John Denver

It's

fun-ny how you sound as if you're right next door____ when you're

real-ly half a world__ a-way.____ I

just can't seem to find the words I'm look-ing for,____ to

*Melody phrased somewhat freely.

say the things that I want to say. ——— I

can't re-mem-ber when I felt so close to you, —— it's

al-most more than I can bear, —— Though I seem a half a mil-lion

miles from you, —— you are in my heart and liv-ing there. —— And the

D / **E**   **G** / **A**   **D** / **E**   **Bm** / **C#m**

mf

moon and the stars ___ are the same ___ ones you see, ___ it's the

Em / **F#m**   **A7** / **B7**   (small notes 2nd time)   **D** / **E**   **A7** / **B7**

same old sun up in the sky. ___ And your / And your

D / **E**   **G** / **A**   **D** / **E**   **Bm** / **C#m**

voice in my ear ___ is like heav - en to me, ___ } like the
face in my dreams ___ is like heav - en to me, ___

Em / **F#m**   **A7** / **B7**   **D** / **E**   *To Coda* ⊕

breez - es here in old Shang - hai. ___

41

There are lov-ers who walk___ hand in hand___ in the park,___ and lov-ers who walk___ all a - lone.___ There are lov-ers who lie___ un-a-fraid___ in the dark,___ and lov - ers who long ____ for home. I

could - n't leave you e - ven if I want - ed to, ____ you're

in my dreams and al - ways near, ____ And es - pec-'ly when I sing the songs I

wrote for you, ____ you are in my heart and liv - ing there. ____ And the

Coda

Em / F#m   F#m / G#m   Bm / C#m

Shang - hai breez - es, cool and clear - ing,

G / A   A7 / B7   D / E

eve - ning's sweet ___ ca - ress, ___

Em / F#m   F#m / G#m   D / E

Shang - hai breez - es soft and gen - tle re -

G / A   Em / F#m   A7 / B7

mind me of ___ your ten - der - ness. ___ And the

moon and the stars_ are the same_ ones you see,_ it's the same old sun up in the sky._

— And your love in my life_ is like heav - en to me,_ like the

breez - es here in old Shang - hai._ And the _ Just like the

slightly held back

breez - es here in old Shang - hai.

slower

Islands

Words and Music by
John Denver

1. Is - lands call out to me like the high - lands___ that
2. Instrumental ___

I al - ways see in my dreams of home; ___ I am nev - er a - lone when I'm

there. ___

Is - lands like
Is - lands be -

so man - y dreams are like can - yons___ but off the main - stream. And there's
long to the sea like the dark signs___ of my mem - o - ry. When the

* Melody slightly simplified throughout

no one there; _____ The dream-er is al - ways a - lone. _____

morn-ing comes _____ they are step - ping stones _____ to the sun. _____

_____ And the might - y blue o - cean keeps roll - ing on ev - 'ry

shore _____ Like the spir - it that binds us to -

geth - er, we are so much more _____ than

is - lands.

(Inst.)

is - lands

(Inst.)

Repeat and fade

Heart To Heart

Words and Music by
John Denver

Slowly

p smoothly

Guitar → (Capo up 2 frets)

Piano →

| D | A | G | Bm | Em |
| E | B | A | C#m | F#m |

hav-en't seen all there is to see, But I've seen quite a bit. I've seen

| Em | D | Em | G | A |
| F#m | E | F#m | A | B |

things I'll al-ways re-mem-ber, Some things I wish that I could for-get. I

| D | A | G | Bm | Em |
| E | B | A | C#m | F#m |

hav-en't quite been a-round the world, But I've been a-round the block; I know that dis - tanc - es_____ are mean-ing-less,_ Like the hands that move_ a - round_ the clock. And I

know that love is ev - 'ry - where,_ Al - ways safe, al - ways true, And ex -

act - ly where_ it comes from Is where it's go - ing to._____ Your heart to mine,_

mf

My heart to yours,_____

Talk a-bout o - pen-ing win - dows, Talk a-bout o - pen-ing doors. My heart to yours,

Your heart to mine,

Love is the light that shines from heart to heart.

Easier

Here I am sit-ting in old Hong Kong With the har-bor and the lights; They're like

dia-monds in the heav-ens, E-nough to bright-en the dark-est nights. There's an-

oth-er side to sor-row As there is to ev-'ry-thing, Like the

oth-er side of lone-ly Is fall-ing in love a-gain. And then you know that there's an an - swer To the suf - fer - ing ___ you see, ___ And

tho' it is - n't eas - y, It's still as sim - ple as you and me. And you

know that love is ev - 'ry - where, ___ Al - ways safe, al - ways true, And ex -

act - ly where ___ it comes from ___ Is where it's go - ing to. ___ Your heart to mine. ___

My heart to yours,___ Talk a-bout o - pen-ing win-dows,

Talk a-bout o - pen-ing doors, My heart to yours,___ Your heart_ to mine,___

1.2.

Love is the light___ that shines___ from heart to heart.___ Your heart to mine_

3. Love is the light___ that shines___ from heart to heart._
cresc.   f

Perhaps Love

Slowly, in tempo

Words and Music by
John Denver

Per-haps love is like a rest-ing place, A shel-ter from the storm, It ex-ists to give you com-fort, It is there to keep you warm, And in those times of trou-ble When you are most a-lone, The mem-o-ry of love will bring you home. Per-haps love is like a win-dow, Per-haps an o-pen door,____ It in-

vites you to come clos-er, It wants to show__you more.____ And

e-ven if you lose your-self And don't know what to do,____ The

mem-o-ry____ of love will__ see you through. Oh

love to some__ is like a cloud,__ to some as__ strong__ as steel, For

some a way__ of liv - ing, For some a way__ to feel, And

some say love is hold - ing on,__ And some say let - ting go,__ And

some say love__ is ev - 'ry - thing, And some say__ they don't know... Per - haps

slightly held back

love is like the o-cean, Full of con-flict, full of change, Like a

in tempo

fire___ when it's cold___ out - side,___ Or thun - der when it rains.___ If

I should live for - ev - er And all my dreams come true, My

mem - o - ries ___ of love will ___ be of you.

slowing

Children Of The Universe

Words and Music by
John Denver and Joe Henry

Slowly

p

(with pedal)

A

Cmaj7

Gm7 3fr.

her - i - tage___ of vi - sion   Was   giv - en to us all _____   To smell the ros - e's fra - grance   To hear the song - bird call —   To

watch the dis - tant moon - light fill —   The com - ing of — the tides —   To

un - der - stand — that life — is more — Than   al - ways — choos - ing

sides —   And

some have seen_ what can_ be seen_ Of sail-ing ships_ and kings_ And

some are giv-en feet of clay_ And some are giv-en wings_

Some must strug-gle just_ to breathe_ Some have a gold-en spoon And

some will nev-er leave_ the nest_ While some walk_ on the

moon _____ And

don't you know_ the life_ that lives_ With-in _____ the si-lent hills _____ Is

just as rich_ and beau-ti-ful _____ And just as un-ful-filled _____ As

man with all_ his in-tel-lect _____ His rea-son and his choice Oh who's to say___ the night - in - gale___ Has an - y less___ a voice___

The

sil - ver dol - phins twist___ and dance___ And sing to___ one an - oth - er The

cos - mic o - cean knows no bounds___ For all that___ live are broth - ers_____ The whip-poor-will, ___ the griz-zly bear ___ The el-e-phant, ___ the whale All

chil-dren of ___ the un-i-verse ___ All weav-ers of the tale ___

So

pal-o-mi-no lie back down ___ And dream your-self to sleep The hawk flies with the mourn-ing dove The li - on with the sheep As

far a - way as you may go We'll nev - er be a - part It's

in your dreams that you will know The sea - sons of the heart

MORE

JOHN DENVER FOLIOS

Aerie All the songs from the album including *Friends With You, Casey's Last Ride, The Eagle And The Hawk.*
#9007 $3.95

An Evening With John Denver All 23 songs from the popular double album including *Annie's Song, Grandma's Feather Bed, Sweet Surrender, Rocky Mountain High* plus 12 pages of color photos.
#9002 $7.95

Autograph This attractive matching folio includes 11 great songs; *Autograph, American Child, Dancing With The Mountains, Whalebones and Crosses* plus full color lyric spread.
#9015 $6.95

Back Home Again Colorful matching folio includes John's hits; *Annie's Song,* the title tune, *Back Home Again, Thank God I'm A Country Boy* and *Sweet Surrender.*
#9004 $5.95

A Christmas Together John Denver And The Muppets Matching folio to the holiday album features *Silent Night, The Twelve Days of Christmas, Have Yourself A Merry Little Christmas, The Peace Carol* plus color pictures and an 8 page lyric section.
#9014 $5.95

Farewell Andromeda All the songs from the album and more from John's T.V. Special *Big Horn; I'd Rather Be A Cowboy, Rocky Mountain Suite, Angels From Montgomery,* plus color photos.
#9006 $5.95

I Want To Live Matching folio containing 11 great songs including *How Can I Leave You Again, I Want To Live, Bet On The Blues* and *Singing Skies And Dancing Waters.*
#9012 $5.95

JD John Denver Matching folio includes *Sweet Melinda, You're So Beautiful, Johnny B. Goode.* 11 songs in all plus full color photos.
#9013 $6.95

John Denver Anthology Piano Vocal A superb volume of over 80 of Denver's best-loved songs; *Rocky Mountain High, Sunshine On My Shoulders, Annie's Song, Country Love, Take Me Home, Country Roads.* Features biography, photos and John Denver's thoughts behind many of the songs.
#9017 $14.95

John Denver's Greatest Hits Matching folio to smash LP contains *Sunshine On My Shoulders, Take Me Home, Country Roads, Follow Me,* plus photos and lyric sheets.
#9010 $6.95

John Denver's Greatest Hits-Vol. 2 Matching folio to the gold album features *Annie's Song, Fly Away, Calypso, I'm Sorry, Back Home Again, Welcome To My Morning.*
#9011 $6.95

The John Denver Songbook Deluxe selection from John's first four best selling albums; *Take Me Home, Country Roads, Poems, Prayers And Promises, My Sweet Lady,* plus photos, woodprints and autobiographical notes.
#9003 $7.95

Rocky Mountain Christmas All the songs from the great seasonal LP plus more Christmas favorites including *Silver Bells, Rudolph The Red Nosed Reindeer, A Baby Just Like You, The Christmas Song.*
#9009 $4.95

Rocky Mountain High Matching folio to the album containing *Goodbye Again, For Baby (For Bobbie), The Season Suite* and *Rocky Mountain High.*
#9005 $5.95

Some Days Are Diamonds Matching folio contains 10 arrangements including the title tune *Some Days Are Diamonds, The Cowboy And The Lady, Country Love,* plus photos and lyric section.
#9016 $6.95

Spirit Matching the hit LP, folio contains *Like A Sad Song, Wrangell Mountain Song, It Makes Me Giggle,* plus full color photos.
#9008 $5.95

Windsong Full color photos and lyric sheets enhance this matching folio to the gold album. Songs include *Calypso, Windsong, Fly Away, Looking for Space* and *I'm Sorry.*
#9001 $5.95

Obtainable at your local music dealer or by sending check or money order to:

WINTER HILL MUSIC Ltd. • P.O. Box 430 • PORT CHESTER, NY 10573

(Please add $1.00 Postage and handling plus sales tax where applicable). Free catalogue available upon request.